MW00904973

Get Me Off
the Treadmill!

Using Ordinary Magic to
Live an Extraordinary Life

Valerie F. MacLeod, M.B.A.

© Copyright 2004 Valerie MacLeod. All rights reserved.

No part of this publication may be reproduced, stored in a retrieval system, or transmitted, in any form or by any means, electronic, mechanical, photocopying, recording, or otherwise, without the written prior permission of the author.

Printed in Victoria, Canada

Note for Librarians: a cataloguing record for this book that includes Dewey Classification and US Library of Congress numbers is available from the National Library of Canada. The complete cataloguing record can be obtained from the National Library s online database at: www.nlc-bnc.ca/amicus/index-e.html
ISBN 1-4120-1693-2

TRAFFORD

This book was published   on-demand in cooperation with Trafford Publishing.
On-demand publishing is a unique process and service of making a book available for retail sale to the public taking advantage of on-demand manufacturing and Internet marketing. On-demand publishing   includes promotions, retail sales, manufacturing, order fulfilment, accounting and collecting royalties on behalf of the author.

Suite 6E, 2333 Government St., Victoria, B.C. V8T 4P4, CANADA
Phone   250-383-6864   Toll-free 1-888-232-4444 (Canada & US)
Fax   250-383-6804   E-mail   sales@trafford.com
Web site www.trafford.com   TRAFFORD PUBLISHING IS A DIVISION OF TRAFFORD HOLDINGS LTD.
Trafford Catalogue #03-2070   www.trafford.com/robots/03-2070.html

10   9   8   7   6   5   4   3

To an extraordinary life...

ABOUT THE AUTHOR

Valerie MacLeod, M.B.A.

Valerie MacLeod is a skilled and insightful facilitator and coach. She is passionate about helping people to *"plan their work and work their plan"*. Her grounded and dynamic coaching adds value by uncovering purpose, sharpening focus on *"the big picture"* and providing clients with the tools they need to achieve success on their own.

"My goal is to help people find their own answers," says Valerie. "My strength lies in asking the right questions."

Valerie specializes in group facilitation and team dynamics. The tools she marshals for her clients include: strategic planning and implementation; change management; teambuilding; motivation; strategy alignment; performance management; and innovation. She works with individuals, executives, teams and organizations to clarify and achieve vision, values and strategies.

Valerie is a Partner with *The Centre for Strategic Management*, a global alliance of diverse Master Consultants, where she is Strategic Planning Practice Leader and a member of the Executive for North America. Valerie has an M.B.A. in human resources organizational development from the University of Calgary and a Bachelor of Mathematics from the University of Waterloo. She lives in Calgary with her husband, Frank, and her two cats, Riffy and T-Bear.

Contact the author through her website: www.valeriemacleod.com.

ACKNOWLEDGMENTS

It is with deep gratitude that I would like to thank the following people for their generous contributions to my life and the gifts of wisdom and magic that went into the creation of this book: Andrew, Chris, Frank, Hazel, Helen, Liz, Jim, Martin and Pat for allowing me to share their inspiring stories; Steve Haines, President of *The Centre for Strategic Management*, for his depth of generosity; My parents, Jack and Jennine MacLeod, for their unconditional love; And my husband, Frank Kurucz, for making each day more full of magic and love than the day before.

CONTENTS

1

Introduction:

The Meaning of Magic

Introduction:

The Meaning of Magic

Let knowledge grow from more to more,
But more of reverence in us dwell;
That mind and soul, according well,
May make one music as before.

– Lord Alfred Tennyson

Human beings are more than the sum of the different segments that make up their lives. Fully living all of the basic components of your life - *physical, intellectual and spiritual* - creates magic. There is magic in integrating all the parts of the Self. There is magic in living a fully integrated life.

I am passionate about helping people *"plan their work and work their plan."* I believe that creating a plan to live a fully integrated life – with all the pieces moving together like a finely tuned musical instrument – is only part of the recipe for success. The most important part of the process is not necessarily in formulating a plan (a recipe), nor in thinking about doing something (lining up the ingredients on the kitchen counter), but in taking *action* to live the plan, to bake the cake, to take the risks, to start the adventure, to create magic.

Get Me Off the Treadmill! is written to assist you in living a more conscious existence – by getting you off the treadmill of life and putting that energy into creating the Extraordinary Life you were meant to live. I have nothing against treadmills. I have one in my basement for exercise, but I do not delude myself that I have moved anywhere in the hour I worked out. The treadmill is exactly in the same position on the floor as it was the previous day. If you want to achieve more in your life than just going through the motions on a treadmill, if you want to discover your purpose and use it to live a fuller life, then this book is for you.

I believe that each of us has a purpose, a reason why we were put on the planet. I also believe that we have the talents and skills to fulfill that purpose.

When I decided to leave my job at a large oil company, it was frightening. I was choosing to follow my purpose, create my own magic, by setting up my own consulting practice after being part of a multinational company. While it was daunting to create a plan to live a balanced life and launch a successful business, implementing it and watching the "magic" occur has been exciting. I now earn more money and I work fewer hours than I did at my old employer.

An added bonus is that as a consultant I get to say "no" to things that don't take me where I want to go – and that isn't usually an option when you are an employee. I truly have *"planned my work and worked my plan"* to create *"magic"* – the life I desire to be living.

This book has been written to help you achieve clarity on what is important to you and harmonize the facets of your life. **Get Me off the Treadmill!** will also take you through the steps to put the plan into practice – work the plan – and create your own unique blend of magic.

What Does Magic Mean to Me?

It means that my life is exciting and full of possibilities, with all the components working effortlessly together. It means that everyday I unmask the magic that is around me – the magic in my niece' laughter, the magic in the colors of the rainbow, the magic in listening – really listening – when my husband tells me about his day and the magic in a stranger's face because of a smile that I share. If you desire magic in your life, take the first step – turn the pages of this book and invest time in creating a full and abundant life for yourself.

I understand that completing a plan to live an Extraordinary Life and putting that plan into action may seem like a difficult task. Allow John D. Rockefeller III's words serve as a beacon of hope: *"The road to happiness lies in two simple principles: find what it is that interests you and that you can do well, and when you find it, put your whole soul into it – every bit of energy and ambition and natural ability you have."* To this end and to help you achieve success, I have included examples from my life and from others' experiences to show you the possibilities and to give you inspiration. You can also refer to the completed *Extraordinary Life Plan* in **Appendix A** as an example and a guide.

Let the magic begin!

2

Extraordinary Life Planning:

The Magic of Balance

Get Me Off the Treadmill!

Extraordinary Life Planning:

The Magic of Balance

Live a balanced life – learn some and think some and
draw and paint and sing and dance and
play and work every day some.

- Robert Fulghum

I admire many people in this world. They aren't necessarily rich or famous, but they are *"whole"* people. All the varied and segmented parts of their lives are integrated into one cohesive, holistic being. They don't behave like one person at their place of employment or schooling, another person with their friends and still another with their family. These people have learned to harmonize the many facets of their life. The people that I admire are confident of where they are going. They are certain of what's important to them and what isn't important, and they take action and make those important dreams happen.

What is Balance?

Balance does not mean doing everything on my list within a certain amount of time. The magic of balance is about making choices regarding what is important to me and balancing those important roles and tasks. It is about saying no, with grace, to requests that aren't aligned with my purpose. Being in balance ensures that I am making a contribution to my part of the world because I am committed and focused. The magic of balance frees up time for me to spend time with my family and friends without guilt because I know they are more important than cleaning up my desk or reading my latest magazine.

People that live a balanced life may not have the perfect balance every day – but each phase of their life has equilibrium. They may put one part of their life on the "back burner" during a certain time period, but as they move into the next phase of their life, they turn up the heat on the part that was "simmering." More energy and time are now invested in this life segment.

When I was working on my MBA several years ago, I was married and working full time. For those three years my social life was almost non-existent, but after I graduated I went on a six-week trip to Australia and New Zealand. When I came back, I once again started seeing friends, attending the theatre and socializing more than when I was a student. If you looked only at the MBA years, you would say that my life was out of balance, but you would realize that I did achieve balance if you looked at the years including and surrounding that period.

Balance should be looked at in blocks of time. You may strive for balance each week – devoting the time you deem as close to the ideal in terms of the physical, intellectual and spiritual areas of your life. You may look at a month as the block of time for achieving your balance – perhaps putting time into volunteering or service at the end of the month to attain this balance.

It is also possible to view blocks of time for balance in larger chunks, such as 10 years. This time span could be divided into phases, for example for five years you may work on a consuming project at work that takes up a large portion of your waking hours, then for the next five years you may transfer to a less taxing assignment so that you can take on primary care of the children, travel or write a book. Whatever block of time you want to define for balance is fine – as long as you have a plan that you are deliberately following to achieve equilibrium over that timespan.

Get Me Off the Treadmill! will help you balance the many roles and segments of your life. It will assist you to determine what is important to you and help you to create and implement plans to ensure you achieve what you most desire. It will help you live "deliberately" and "purposefully." By creating and following your plan for an Extraordinary Life, you will take control of your life, not just "take up space on the planet." You will discover and live your own special magic.

Freud was once asked what he thought a normal person should be able to do well. He said, "Lieben und arbeiten" (to love and to work). Perhaps this answer seems surprisingly simple, but it effectively sums up what most of us feel to be important – a holistic approach to life: having the physical, intellectual and spiritual parts of your life working together in harmony.

Out of Balance

When people are out of balance they often don't see the signs. They could be far along the road to burnout before they take a fresh look at their life. There are many signs of imbalance including: you are making poor decisions compared to decisions in the past, your relationships are not running as smoothly as they used to, you are experiencing health problems or your performance is below your usual standards. Are you running on empty? Are you running on caffeine?

When you are in balance, all the pieces of your life work together harmoniously. You have an almost endless amount of energy. Everything flows effortlessly.

Purposes of "Get Me Off the Treadmill!"

Get Me Off the Treadmill! unfolds with three purposes in mind:
1. To help you define that which is important for you to achieve this harmonious, Extraordinary Life
2. To assist you to create and implement a plan to help you pull the pieces together into a cohesive, effective whole
3. To help you to continually experience the magic of a balanced life

The Approach

I will use *The Centre for Strategic Management's* Systems Thinking Approach^SM as the model to help you achieve the purposes of this book. The model is described in detail in **Appendix B**. We will concentrate on the five main areas of the model:

1. *Defining an Extraordinary Life - If I'm not on a treadmill what am I doing?*
2. *Tracking Progress – Am I moving ahead? Am I on the right road?*
3. *Creating Strategies – What should I do to create magic?*
4. *Ensuring Success – How do I use ordinary magic to live an Extraordinary Life?*
5. *Remembering the Outside World – How will external changes affect me?*

While important, the *creation* of a plan to integrate the many parts of your life into a satisfying whole isn't of primary significance. More critical is that we live that plan – that we put it into action. You would be better advised to create a mediocre plan that you live than to come up with a terrific strategy that gets ignored.

Helen

Helen, a friend of mine since high school, lives an Extraordinary Life. Her life is balanced among the physical, intellectual and spiritual areas. She is a successful manager at a large financial organization and an active rock climber, skier, and snowboarder, amongst other sports, and still finds time to volunteer in her community. In fact, she was recently loaned by her company to the United Way to help organize numerous workplace fundraising campaigns. She has close relationships with her partner, family and friends and even with her ex-husband. Her avocations include reading voraciously, writing and performing music in a band and co-producing videos and films.

Helen isn't Superwoman, at least not by her standards. She's made conscious choices that have allowed her to fully express the many dimensions of her life. For example, she does not spend a lot of time watching television or shopping for matching shoes, nor does she get bogged down in small worries - she purposefully lives simply and somewhat spartanly. Helen regularly practices "clearing out the clutter," both physically and mentally, which helps her maintain the time and energy to stay connected. For Helen, connecting to the spiritual realm means taking time to explore her inner self and her motivations through meditation, journal entries and by simply and consciously enjoying the simple things in life.

Like everyone else, Helen has her share of ups and downs. She finds it particularly beneficial to recall a special dream that she had many years ago in which she encountered a female Buddha and a very bright light. My friend regularly contemplates this dream as it reminds her to live carefully, contemplatively and respectfully and to have patience with herself and others. Her approach seems to be working: recently, she was awarded the "Spiritual Leader" award by her staff!

Three Parts of Life – *Physical, Intellectual and Spiritual*

There are numerous ways to define the pieces of a balanced life. I decided to go for familiar definitions – physical, intellectual and spiritual.

The **Physical** aspect is the "doing" facet of our lives. This part is easiest for others to understand because the behaviors and results can be seen. We all play many roles in the physical facet of our lives: spouse, parent, sibling, worker, friend, child, student, homemaker, grandparent or volunteer. The **Physical** facet includes health, wealth, career, family and community.

Our **Intellectual** facet includes the "thinking" aspects of life. As students, we take courses that challenge and expand our thinking, so this aspect of our lives is easily understood.

The final part of this trio is the **Spiritual** facet. This is the part of life where people usually spend the least amount of time. It is the "being" aspect of life. The spiritual component is our connection to something beyond us. We fill up our internal well of energy and ideas through connecting with our spirit.

Living in balance between the **physical, intellectual and spiritual** facets of your life is magical. It allows you to get off the treadmill and start living the Extraordinary Life you were meant to live.

3

Remembering the Outside World:

How Will External Changes Affect Me?

Remembering the Outside World:

How Will External Changes Affect Me?

I hold that man is in the right
who is most closely in league with the future

- Henrik Ibsen

Life would be so much easier if I didn't have to contend with the outside world, if I could live my life without concern for things and people outside of me. Experiencing magic everyday is simple if I didn't have to manage my investments in an unstable market, commute through heavy traffic, attend communication meetings at the school, celebrate family birthdays or spend time recycling. However, I do live in a world that is impacted by outside situations and individuals so we are going to take the external world into consideration.

You will remember the outside world by:
- Learning more about your issues and barriers
- Discovering patterns in your life
- Identifying Key People to support your plan
- Conducting an External Scan

Getting Ready

The description Extraordinary Life may be frightening to some of you. I know it was to me when I first thought about it. Extraordinary? Me? But my gifts and talents are different from yours, I am not exactly the same as everyone else, I am unique. My Extraordinary Life is lived by my definition of extraordinary, not anyone else's standard. Extraordinary to me is every day working towards realizing my mission, living my values and maintaining balance. Living the magic of an Extraordinary Life means that I know where I am going and understand what steps I must follow to achieve that desired life. It means that I am clear about what I want to achieve and be. Striving for my desired life helps bring simplicity because I am clearer about what I want to do and not do, I can more easily say "no" to the clutter that used to fill my house and life. Living an Extraordinary Life allows me to move from "living to work" to "working to live."

You will begin your journey to an Extraordinary Life by understanding a little more about yourself as well as the world in which you live. If you think about living an integrated life rather than a splintered one, you will begin to distribute your time and energy differently. If you are conscious of moving towards an Extraordinary Life, you will think differently about the choices in your life.

Critical Issues

I want you to think about the issues that are in the front of your mind, the things that you worry about or think about. Are you concerned about the future of your career, the difficulty of returning to school, how a change in salary will affect your lifestyle, caring for aging parents, finding good employees or balancing your children's activities with finding time for yourself?

Knowing these critical issues will be useful when we create strategies later in the planning process, because these burning concerns must be handled as part of your **Extraordinary Life Plan**.

To define your critical issues, write the answers to these questions:

- What are the things that worry you?

- What keeps you awake at night?

- What are the critical issues in your life?

Barriers

Sometimes I am my own worst enemy when it comes to achieving what I desire. I subconsciously (and sometimes consciously) put roadblocks and barriers in my way. I made many excuses for not finishing this book: I was busy, it was too difficult to write at the office because of the phone and email, it was impossible to work at home because of all the things I needed to do at home and I had lost the drive. The truth is, I am afraid of failure. If I didn't complete the book, then no one would be able to say I was a failure if it didn't sell well. I put up barriers that seemed like logical reasons for not finishing the manuscript. However, they were impediments to my achieving what I really wanted: to help people discover how to get off the treadmill and how to live Extraordinary Lives.

We all put up barriers in our lives. Why would we do this? Usually because it is more comfortable to stay where we are than to take risks and make changes. It is easier to remain in an environment we know rather than step out into the unknown.

These barriers can be powerful, but we can rob them of their power by acknowledging and understanding them. Examples of barriers include fear of failure, not enough time/money/energy, uncertainty about what we want, a history of failures and being too busy keeping up with life to plan.

I once worked with a team that used water as a metaphor for their planning process. Water always finds a way to overcome any barriers in its path. Water goes over, under, around or through barriers. So when this group spoke about "being like water," they meant they were overcoming the barriers in their path. I want you to think about how you can become "like water" to overcome your barriers. In order to finish this book I examined my barriers and decided the best way to counter them was to get away from all the interruptions at work and home and rediscover my passion for writing the book. I spent a week in the Rocky Mountains walking, thinking and typing. My excuses were gone and I was able to move ahead with joy.

Pat

A business associate of mine left a large communications company to become a self-employed consultant. Pat definitely had some barriers to creating a successful consulting practice. Many of her contacts were in her former organization; her husband worked away from home for extended periods of time; she felt she was abandoning an organization which had treated her very well for 24 years; she had no experience in marketing; and she had no administrative help.

However, she discovered one of her most surprising barriers involved visualization. She had visualized and created affirmations to successfully leave her long-term career and transform herself into a successful businessperson. Unfortunately, she forgot to visualize herself successfully handling the transition from the corporate world to entrepreneurship.

Until Pat dealt with the missing pieces, she found herself thinking each day was simply like a day off from the corporate job. Eventually she was successful by creating a vision to handle the transition to self-employment and following a plan to achieve that vision.

Identify your barriers by answering these questions:

- What barriers, roadblocks, fears, limitations, walls, defenses, obstacles and/or expectations do you have about living an Extraordinary Life?

- What is stopping you from living the life you desire today?

We will bring this list back into our planning later in the book.

Decision Making Questionnaire

We sometimes make decisions in life without understanding the underlying reasons for those choices. As we grow and develop, these primary motivations may change, or the basic need we are meeting could remain the same over time.

Answer the self -questionnaire below to help you understand some of the reasons you make decisions:

- What are the most important decisions you have made in your life?

- What were the significant events or "turning points" in your life?

- What people have influenced you most?

- What tasks or activities do you most enjoy? What are the tasks or activities that when you are involved in them "time flies"?

- What do you least enjoy doing? Why?

- How would you define success?

- What are you most proud of doing or achieving? Why?

Review your answers to the above questions. Document the patterns you see in your answers:

What do these patterns in your answers tell you?

Key People

The **Key People** in your life have very definite impacts on the choices you make. They can either support you in making the changes you will discover are necessary for your Extraordinary Life, or they can hinder you in going for your goals. These Key People can include your family, co-workers, friends, your boss, teachers, spiritual advisors, coaches or professional counselors.

In addition to my wonderful husband, my business partners at *The Centre for Strategic Management* and my husband's family, I created a "surrogate" family of close friends because my own family lives many miles away from me. These Key People support me when I am down, celebrate my successes, share the magic and help me maintain balance.

Who are the Key People in your life that you would like to receive support from when you implement changes to create magic in your life? These are the people with whom you'll share your plan and whose help you'll ask for when you are trying new behaviors or creating new patterns. They will encourage you when you are discouraged and rejoice with you when you are successful. You want to choose people who will give you support, talk to you "straight" and challenge your assumptions. There are already enough barriers in our lives, so do not ask for support from people who you know will hinder your progress or try to drag you down.

Write the names of these supportive Key People in your life:

We will incorporate the names of these people when we create our feedback strategies to ensure successful implementation of our plan.

Future External Scanning

Do you remember experimenting in your high school science class by placing a large glass bell over an open flame? The flame went out when the oxygen in the system was used up. This is an example of a closed system, which means a lack of new oxygen entering the system extinguished the flame.

However, we don't live and work in a closed system, in isolation from other people and events in the world. There is no glass wall preventing intrusions into the system we call life. Therefore, we can be impacted by changes in the outside world over which we have little or no influence. For example, I am saving for my retirement through different investments. Events as major as a stock market crash or as minor as a rumor about one of the companies that I hold can affect me. Neither of these events has anything to do with me as an individual, but they can impact how I live my retirement years to a greater or lesser extent.

In order to appreciate some of the events that might happen in the outside world, you will conduct regular future **External Scans**. These will help you understand and anticipate future external happenings so that you can either take advantage of or lessen the impact of them. An External Scan is focused on the future – trends, patterns, movements that could occur to you or are happening to other groups of people that might impact you in the future.

An External Scan is a tool to get you thinking about some of these potential outside events in order to successfully live an Extraordinary Life. Don't worry if you don't know how to categorize an event; just use the External Scan as a way for broadening your thinking about what you need to consider when creating and living your **Extraordinary Life Plan**.

External Scan - SKEPTIC Analysis

At *The Centre for Strategic Management* we use the acronym SKEPTIC to conduct a future External Scan of events that could occur in the future.

S	**Socio-demographic** • What future changes in age, migration or hobbies are of impact or interest to you? These changes can be in your life or the lives of other people like your clients, family or community members. Examples: your children graduating from school; entering or leaving prime child-bearing age; changing attitudes of employees; young people moving out of your community; aging parents.
K	**Competition** • Who might be out there in the future doing the same tasks as you at work, at home, at school, in the family or in your volunteer association? • Who might compete for the same resources, time, affection or space? Examples: other companies in the same industry; other arts, community or charity groups; government agencies; your children; other employees.
E	**Environmental/Economic** • What could happen economically that you should be aware of? • What upcoming environmental issues should you track? Examples: rising housing costs; increased fuel costs; a possible new wildlife preserve; changing interest and mortgage rates; global warming; recycling; water rationing.
P	**Political** • Are there any potential political changes that could impact you? Examples: retirement of your company president; elections; new groups being formed around issues.
T	**Technology/Technical** • How can changes in technology affect the achievement of an Extraordinary Life? • What potential technical changes to things you do or to tools you might use should you watch? Examples: new products from outside the country; a lapse of patent or copyright; faster internet connections; miniaturization of products; maturation of products.
I	**Industry/Substitutes** • What is happening or could happen in your field of work, play or study? Examples: merger of two associations or organizations; addition of new courses in your field of study; your company is a possible takeover target; the need to upgrade your skills; adoption of new equipment; additional training requirements; appointment of a new leader.
C	**Customer/Client/Constituent/Community/Family/Friends** • Who do you serve? For whom do you create value? Whose life do you make better or easier? How might their needs and lives change in the future? Examples: your family is becoming more independent; customers in your geographical area are using global suppliers; people are getting too busy to care about issues.

Your Future External Scan

Take some time to write down potential future changes in these areas that could impact you living an Extraordinary Life:

S	
K	
E	
P	
T	
I	
C	

4

Defining an Extraordinary Life:

If I'm Not on a Treadmill, What Am I Doing?

Defining an Extraordinary Life:

If I'm Not on a Treadmill, What Am I Doing?

The future is not some place we are going to,
but one we are creating.
The paths to it are not found, but made
and the activity of making them
changes both maker and destination.

- John Schaar

In order for me to get off the treadmill I must know what I am getting instead. At the present time the treadmill might be getting me nowhere but at least it is familiar. The alternative to the treadmill must be compelling enough for me to make changes in my life, big ones and small ones.

Getting off the treadmill for me meant that I was giving up security, a job I liked and people I enjoyed working with. However, I also knew that my days were not filled with **magic**, that they were ordinary. I had to create an alternative to the treadmill that was exciting for me to make the **"leap of faith"** off the treadmill. I created that alternative by dreaming up what I could be doing and how I could be using my talents in a way that delighted my clients and thrilled me.

The Alternative to the Treadmill – *Your Ideal Future*

You are going to create your alternative to the treadmill in this chapter. You will define what an Extraordinary Life looks like for you. **Your Ideal Future** is where you want to be at some point in the future. It is what you want to be when you experience **magic** every day, when you achieve your dream.

For the time being, ignore questions about *how* you will get to Your Ideal Future. I know this may not be comfortable for you, but put aside for now those doubts about not being able to achieve your desires. Later, we'll be more practical. For now, though, give yourself permission to dream, to release your pent-up desires about your future.

Navigation - *What Do I Want My Life to Be Like?*

Your Ideal Future will give you a place on a roadmap by which to navigate and make choices. When you are making a difficult decision, you will compare it against Your Ideal Future. You will ask if this choice will move you closer to the life you want. If the answer is yes, then follow that path. Using Your Ideal Future as a checkpoint for decisions ensures that you will make choices that keep you on the right path.

For example, I was asked to join a small consulting firm. This option had many positives: I would be working with people I liked, I would have more administrative support and I would receive a regular paycheck. However, it would move me away from my Ideal Future of successful self-employment, flexibility and balance. I decided to decline the offer based upon the answer to the question: "Will this choice move me closer to my definition of an Extraordinary Life?"

Your Ideal Future can be your guiding star. Sailors used the North Star to guide them through the choppy ocean waters, allowing them to navigate their course with confidence. The sailors, of course, never actually reached the North Star. Many of us will not get to our Ideal Future within the time frame we set. But like those sailors, if we use our Ideal Future as our guiding star for making decisions, then we are closer to reaching our Ideal Future than if we had no plan at all. By using Your Ideal Future as your own North Star, you'll be making choices that will put you on course towards the Extraordinary Life you want.

The Ideal Future is different for every person. It is as individual as our fingerprints and our dreams. It will combine the three parts of our lives - *physical, intellectual and spiritual* - into a cohesive whole.

Unconscious Navigation

Having a clear idea of your life's purpose can guide your decision making, sometimes when you don't even realize it. In the early 1990s, I was working for Amoco Petroleum (now BP Energy) and participated in a workshop in which we had to write a description of the ideal day. I wrote about being a successful, self-employed human resources consultant with an office at home, satisfied clients and working mainly in facilitation and training. Then I promptly forgot about it.

In 1996, I was presented with the opportunity to leave the company with a generous package. Without even remembering my previous "ideal day" description, my husband and I talked about the option at length. I decided to go from working for a company to becoming my own boss. About a year after leaving Amoco, I stumbled across my "ideal day" description and was surprised at how close my current situation was to that ideal – right down to the cat sleeping in the corner of the office.

I believe that my "ideal day" was imbedded in my subconscious and it helped keep me focused when I was making my life plans and business decisions. If you have an idea of what you want the future to look like, it is even more powerful and compelling if it is in your conscious mind, instead of tucked away somewhere in your memory.

Sometimes I feel a lack of direction in life, I seem to have little energy for doing things that I "should" do. This often occurs when I'm alone too much because I am a social animal. Instead of being mired in that place, I go for a walk and rethink my Ideal Future – what I want to do with my life and how I want to live my life holistically. Because of the walk and the remembered Ideal Future I create renewed energy to reconnect with the magic and make the right decisions for me.

Knowing our Ideal Future gives us energy when we feel low. It draws us closer with its magnetism – the energy created when our hopes, aspirations, dreams and desires come together. When we need help in any segment of our lives, it provides guidance. Your Ideal Future will help you stay on the road to achieving the life you most desire.

Mission and Values

The **Ideal Future** is comprised of two pieces:

- **Mission**
- **Values**

Mission is our reason for existence. It defines our purpose in life. A clear mission can act like a magnet, pulling you forward when you don't have the energy to take action yourself.

My mission gives me direction, helps me make decisions and acts as an anchor to keep me from floating away with the current of distractions. It defines how I am to use my gifts and abilities for the world.

The second part of Ideal Future is **Values**. Your values are deeply rooted; they make you unique, they guide your behavior and assist you in making choices. Even if you have never defined your values, they are nevertheless part of you and you will subconsciously make decisions based upon them.

When we meet I will interact with you using my values and likewise, you will interact with me using your values. By getting to know me you can see my actions and results and thus, also know my values. My values are a part of who I am, an integral part of what makes me Valerie MacLeod and not someone else.

Mission – *Tapping the Power Within*

Mission defines why you are on the planet. It may not be what you are doing today but it can have an incredible amount of power. It can provide you with energy when you thought your resources were tapped.

I believe that each of us has a unique purpose, a reason for being that is imbedded deep inside of us – in our DNA and in our soul. Knowing your purpose can propel you forward and give you hope. In his book, **Man's Search for Meaning**, Victor Frankl said mission is the one thing that can keep someone alive in a setting as brutal and life threatening as a concentration camp. *"The prisoner who had lost faith in the future – his future – was doomed. With his loss of belief in the future, he also lost his spiritual hold; he let himself decline and became subject to mental and physical decay."*

My mission is to educate, to guide people to discover their own answers. I always knew I was going to be a teacher, as a child I played teacher for hours. My friends and I spent many happy times in the classroom we created in the basement. I never dreamt of being a doctor or an astronaut, I knew what I was going to be. I taught Sunday School, dancing and at summer camp all before I was 16! With the assistance of two of my mathematics teachers I decided to attend their alma mater, University of Waterloo, to become a high school mathematics teacher. However, in my final year of high school I decided that high school math teachers didn't make enough money and stayed in mathematics but switched into computer programming. After graduation I programmed for a few years for two different companies but mainly taught computer courses for them. While studying for my Masters I took one Human Resources course and knew that I should be teaching and facilitating in HR as my career. I spent some time in different parts of HR but was always drawn back to teaching.

Even though part of me knew I was put on the planet to educate, I did not always make decisions in line with that mission because that purpose was not in my consciousness. However, teaching always presented itself to me and I am happiest when helping others discover. If I was more aware of education as my mission, I might have made some different choices along the way. Now that I am consciously aware of my mission, I make choices in line with it.

You may not be as aware of your mission in life but the exercises in this chapter will help you decide the one thing that is most important in your life.

Planning Date

When creating a plan for your life, it is easier to visual that future time by choosing a specific time in the future. It could be:

- A milestone birthday
- The day you retire
- The celebration of a birth or wedding
- The accomplishment of a goal
- Five years from today
- New Year's Day in eight years

It should be at least five years in the future in order to give you a challenging goal to work towards.

Write that date here:

This is the date we will use as our planning horizon. All of our future planning will use this date.

Uncovering Your Mission

Spend time thinking about the answers to these questions. They are prompts to assist you in determining your mission.

What are you passionate about?

What would you do even if you were not paid or rewarded?

When do you most feel the joy of being alive?

How do you want to be remembered?

What are you doing when you are creating magic?

Assume it is the future and there is an article published about you, what would you like the article to highlight about your life's accomplishments?

What challenges are you drawn to?

What talents & skills have you possessed from the beginning?

What are you doing when you are drawing on the best parts of you?

What changes in the world are you called to make?

At a banquet in your honor, what would you like the speaker to say about your contribution to the world?

What would you like to commit your life to doing?

What can you be excellent at for the world?

What accomplishments of yours would you want your grandchildren to be proud of?

Consider two or three people that you admire, what characteristics and deeds do you admire in them?

Review the answers you have written to the questions. What theme exists around your mission?

Your Mission Movie

Play a movie in your mind. It is called "Mission Possible" and you are the star. The movie begins with scenes of your life that you have already experienced. The current scene is you reading this book. The next scenes in the movie are about you living an Extraordinary Life, one full of **magic** where you live a balanced life and fulfill your mission.

Write below what you want the next scenes in your life to be as you live "Mission Possible":

Your Ideal Future Mission

Now take time to review the answers to the questions from *Uncovering Your Mission*. You answered the questions separately, but they need to be combined into one Mission that will then provide you with personal guidance for your journey.

- **Imagine you are living an Extraordinary Life, one where you are living with passion and purpose. Describe that mission in words:**

- **Now describe that same mission in pictures, symbols or colors.** For example, I would draw me in front of a group of adults facilitating them through jointly solving a work problem.

Values – *Living with Authenticity*

Values are the second part of Your Ideal Future and are the principles that guide your daily life. They are so vital to you that if you had to give them up for some reason you would cease to be the person you are today. Your values are an integral part of who you are – they are so deeply rooted in your being that you may not be entirely aware of how to define them, but they define you.

Because values are such an intrinsic part of our lives, often times we are not aware of them. Unconscious of them, they impact our decisions, and that is why we need to spend some time articulating what our values are. We don't usually notice how our values impact our decisions unless they are challenged in some way.

Jim

An associate of mine believed it was necessary to leave his job because he valued treating people respectfully, and he thought this was not being honored in the workplace. He felt that the organization was treating their employees like young horses whose spirits had to be broken before their character could be rebuilt. An extensive program gave colleagues negative feedback in front of their peers in what he felt was a way that did not honor the employee's feelings. After seeing the unintentional results of the program, which included ulcers, sick leave and high stress, Jim left the organization and has never regretted his decision. He knew that living by his values was more important than the paycheck he was receiving from that company.

There are no "right" or "wrong" values. Your values simply exist, having been developed internally as you traveled through your life. Some people call values principles, beliefs or philosophies. Whatever you call them, they define who you are and why you live your life as you do.

My top values are *integrity, balance, personal and professional growth* and *harmony*. They define who I am, how I serve my clients, how I interact with friends and family and how I make decisions.

Values Revealed

During university I attended an informational evening presented by a technology company. Prospective employees, like myself, learned about the organization prior to on-campus interviews. New employees and summer students shared their experiences at the company.

One of the highlights of the evening was stories from some of their new employees about the exciting projects they were working on. I found it interesting that a common pattern emerged about long hours, weekend work and wonderful rewards. Although it sounded exciting, my concern for balance did not allow me to buy into the culture of that organization. I decided not to apply for an interview with that company, and I believe it was the best decision for both of us.

Your Personal Values Inventory

Review the following list of possible values. Add any values that you think are missing. Think carefully about your choices – limit yourself to only five "High" rated values.

Rank the values as High, Medium or Low; "High" being those values that are extremely important to you in your life.

PERSONAL VALUES	H/M/L
Health	
Wealth	
Family Happiness	
Accomplishments	
Autonomy	
Personal Growth	
Contribution	
Integrity	
Recognition	
Respect	
Adventure	
Challenge	
Teamwork	
Enjoyment	
Control	
Stability	
Creativity	
Spirituality	
Responsibility	
Balance	
Professional Growth	
Justice	
Connection	
Harmony	

Based on Core Personal Values, *Successful Career and Life Planning*, Stephen Haines (Crisp Publications, Menlo Park, CA, 2000), p. 32

Using Values

Were you surprised by your choices? We often do not think about our values until we are forced to make choices.

I use my values to make both major and minor decisions: I organize my work week so that I work four days on average because I value balance; I have turned down potential clients, knowing they would be better served by someone who specializes in certain subjects because I want all my dealings to have integrity; and I try to find a common ground in all discussions and conflict because I value harmony.

Need Work?

Which of your core values do you think need some work? In other words, which of the values you have identified as critical would you like to develop more deeply?

Ask the Key People in your life which values they think you could be living more fully. I know this may be difficult to do, especially if you have just defined your values, but getting feedback from people you trust is an excellent way of determining which areas of your life you could improve upon.

Record the core values you would like to work on or develop on a deeper level:

Commitment – *Acting with Conscious Intent*

"The important thing is this:
to be able at any moment to sacrifice what we are
for what we could become."

- Charles Du Bos

Congratulations! You have now completed creating Your Ideal Future by writing your personal mission and values. Do they surprise you, delight you or call to you? Collectively, these components describe the life you want to achieve. You may already be living some of Your Ideal Future, or you may find you have created an entirely new, and hopefully exhilarating, path for yourself.

If you are a visual thinker, you may want to consolidate the parts of Your Ideal Future into a collage or picture. This visual representation of where you want to be can help you stay focused in the time ahead. I have a collage of magazine pictures on the side of my file cabinet in my office. It helps remind me where I am going when I am doing paperwork (which I hate). Place it where you'll see it often – on your office wall, the refrigerator, your mirror, as your screen saver or in your daily planner. Seeing it regularly will assist you in achieving your desired life by reminding you of what's truly important and where you want to be headed.

There is a difference between creating an Ideal Future and committing to it. Commitment is an act of courage where you choose your path with conscious intent. It is an internal act that you reveal through your actions. You can help solidify your commitment by sharing it with others. For some of us, the commitment isn't real until it is publicly shared – then you are truly committed.

Writer W.H. Murray says it best: *"Until one is committed there is hesitancy, the chance to draw back, always ineffectiveness. Concerning all acts of initiative and creation, there is one elementary truth, the ignorance of which kills countless ideas and splendid plans: that the moment one definitely commits oneself, then Providence moves too.*

"All sorts of things occur to help one that would never otherwise have occurred. A whole stream of events issues from the decision, raising in one's favor all manner of unforeseen incidents and meetings and material assistance, which no man could have dreamt would have come his way."

Commitment in Action

When I first started consulting I had a clear vision of working on my own and satisfying clients, but I did not have a clear commitment to an alliance of consultants that I had joined. Not much came out of this alliance with *The Centre for Strategic Management* because without commitment I did not put much effort into it.

At the one year point, I made a declaration to two of my business associates in the alliance: I would give the Centre one year, and if not much happened I would leave the group. I committed to them, to be a full participant in trying to use the models, tools and ideas. Because I made the commitment it changed how dealings went during the next year. I approached people and my work differently. I started getting more work using *The Centre's* Strategic Management work – helping organizations create and implement strategic plans. Now that I was committed and knew what I wanted, I had renewed energy and focus.

I am now a Partner with that alliance - *The Centre for Strategic Management.* I'm on the Executive Committee and am Practice Leader for Strategic Planning for North America. Without that commitment I would have made different choices and would be in a different place – I could still be floating, just surviving. But because I knew where I was going and shared that declaration with others I achieved more than I ever thought I could.

If you want to achieve your dreams you must make a decision, you must commit to those dreams. Only then will you see the opportunities available to reach those dreams through the lenses of opportunity.

Thoughts on Ideal Future

Your Ideal Future helps you determine what you want your Extraordinary Life to look like in the future. It gives you the description of the alternative to the treadmill. This clear idea of where you are going gives you direction and helps you make the decisions that lead you in that direction. A clear idea gives energy, excitement and magic to the journey.

Your Ideal Future is comprised of mission and values. Mission acts like a magnet pulling you towards the life you want to live. Values are the unique aspects of your life that ground you and upon which you, consciously or unconsciously, take action and make decisions.

Review your mission and values with some of the Key People in your life. Based upon their input, make any modifications necessary to your mission and values exercises.

Once you have thought deeply about this key component, take some time to write actions for more fully living your mission and values:

- _____

- _____

- _____

- _____

- _____

- _____

5

Tracking Progress:

Am I Moving Ahead?
Am I On the Right Road?

Tracking Progress:

Am I Moving Ahead?
Am I On the Right Road?

Sometimes the only thing we do to avoid success
is refuse to be energetic on our own behalf.

- Barbara Sher

Measurement is often an area that makes people feel uncomfortable. They wonder how they are going to gauge progress in areas of their lives which don't include hard numbers. Although I agree that it would be easier to ignore Tracking Progress, I do also believe that it is invaluable to showing us where to make adjustments.

Importance of Measurement

Recently I re-learned the importance of measurement. I was getting comfortable with how my life was going and had gotten lax in my measuring of progress towards living an Extraordinary Life. With the assistance of my business coach, we decided to revisit my measures and track them weekly. I discovered that by being diligent in watching some of my "leading" indicators that I could make large changes in my satisfaction levels by making a few small changes in my behavior.

A "leading" indicator, compared to a "lagging" indicator, is a pro-active way of looking at things. Instead of looking at the final result, leading indicators look at something at the beginning of the cycle. For example, a lagging indicator is income; a more telling leading indicator would be client satisfaction. You could do something about client satisfaction prior to it adversely impacting the bottom line. In life, instead of waiting for a large event, you could look at the outcomes along the way. You could measure the amount of one-on-one time you spend with your children as a leading indicator of a good relationship with your children.

For a leading indicator in business, I count the number of contacts I make weekly with existing and potential clients. This is a better indicator of the health of my consulting practice instead of counting the dollars that are generated. In life, I count the number of dates with my husband, where the two of us do something together without anyone else, instead of waiting for an argument to erupt for me to work on the relationship.

Setting Success Measures for living my purpose may not be easy, but the process is important to ensure we aren't standing still. After all, don't we want to make a contribution by living our dreams instead of just taking up space on the earth?

We are now going to quantifiably measure your success in moving towards your Ideal Future. We are going to set Success Measures that indicate whether or not you are achieving what you've set out to accomplish.

Measurement - *How Will I Know I Am Making Progress?*

Measurement is an area that many people try to skip, or postpone. However, it is the only way of really knowing if you are moving towards an Extraordinary Life.

We must answer **Three Critical Questions** in setting our goals:

- How will we know we are successful?
- How will we know we are moving towards or away from success?
- What do we do if we are off course?

Common Errors in Measurement

A common error that people make in setting Success Measures is over measuring. Once they get comfortable with measurement they try to measure everything. I have discovered that both in business and life it is better to measure a few important things instead of measuring everything.

Where Do Success Measures Come From?

Success Measures do not come out of thin air. You will measure your success towards Your Ideal Future. Your Mission and Values determine what you feel is important to measure. Before deciding what to measure I want to recommend areas that you should consider when determining your Success Measures:

There are seven **Key Success Measures** areas that we should consider measuring:

- Health
- Wealth
- Career
- Family
- Community
- Intellectual
- Spiritual

Not everyone will be comfortable with measurement, especially quantifying areas that don't have definite numbers. Here are some examples of Key Success Measures you might gauge. Try to come up with your own Success Measures, though, to measure your own unique progress towards Your Ideal Future.

- **Health – weight, exercise**
- **Wealth – investments, net worth**
- **Career – satisfaction**
- **Family – closeness with spouse and children**
- **Community – volunteering, impact on the environment**
- **Intellectual – development**
- **Spiritual - connectedness**

Possible Success Measures

Review Your Ideal Future from the previous chapter. For each of the seven areas, write down at least one Success Measure that you might gauge over the next three to five years to demonstrate whether you are moving towards your ideal in that area.

Don't worry about *how* to measure, just write what should be tracked in each area. You can also look at my **Extraordinary Life Plan** in the **Appendix A** for more examples of what to measure.

- Health –

- Wealth –

- Career –

- Family –

- Community –

- Intellectual –

- Spiritual –

Your Key Success Measures

Key Success Measures are the few and important measures that show you are making progress towards Your Ideal Future.

Now choose the measures that will be <u>most important</u> for determining whether you are moving toward your dreams. They are the few key measures that will clearly indicate if you are living the life you want to live or are missing the mark. Many people want to measure everything, but try to narrow the list to one or two measurements in each of the seven areas. The total number of Key Success Measures you are evaluating should be ten or less.

When you have tracked your Key Success Measures for a few months you may be able to reduce the number of measures that show you are making progress towards your Extraordinary Life.

Key Success Measures:

1.

2.

3.

4.

5.

6.

7.

8.

9.

10.

Gauging Progress

Success Measures need to be measurable. There are four categories of measurement:

Quality – a subjective perception by the recipient, i.e. the quality of your relationship as perceived by your spouse, your self-perception of the quality of your spiritual life.

Quantity – facts, ratios, percentages, i.e. the number of times you exercise per week, the percentage of body weight reduction.

Time – date or amount of time, i.e. the completion date of your degree or diploma, the amount of time spent reading.

Cost – the monetary value, i.e. annual donations to charity, your income.

Here are some examples of how to measure indicators of success:

- Percentage increase in income
- Number of vacation days spent with family
- Amount of time invested in personal and professional development
- Decrease in debt
- Perceived increase in aerobic ability
- Increase in customer satisfaction tracked by survey results

Creating a Tracking System

Don't wait for your "ship to come in"
and feel angry and cheated when it doesn't.
Get going with something small.

- Irene Kassorla

Now that you've chosen some Key Success Measures to gauge and you understand the various ways you can quantify your goals. Let's create a goal tracking system:

- **Using the Key Success Measures Chart, write your maximum ten Key Success Measures in the "Success Measures" column**
- **Below each key measure, record how you are going to measure each factor. For example, if your key area is community impact, you might measure it by the dollars and time invested per month**
- **In the column on the far right, record the target you want to achieve in that measurement area over the next three to five years**
- **In the column beside the "Target", write the date by which you hope to achieve that target**
- **Complete each row by recording your current status for each measure. See the Key Success Measures chart in Appendix A to assist you in completing your measurement tracking system**

Each of our Key Success Measures will be as unique as we are. You may have the same Key Areas as others, but will choose to measure them differently. For example, one area could be family health. One person may measure family health by the amount of time the family spends together away from the home, while another person may count the number of meals that the family eats together. Neither measurement is right or wrong – it is the right measure if it shows you are making progress towards your ideal life.

Key Success Measures can impact one another and your values. For example, I measure the number of days that I work per week and my monthly consulting income. Because I value balance, I choose to work four days per week. Naturally, this impacts the amount of money I make in a month. I could boost my income by working seven days per week, but then I wouldn't be living my definition of balance. Because Success Measures are not independent from each other, I must make the best choices depending upon the life I want to live that is consistent with my values.

Key Success Measures Chart

Complete the Success Measure Tracking System form as best you can:

Success Measures	Current Status	Target Date	Target
1.			
2.			
3.			
4.			
5.			
6.			
7.			
8.			
9.			
10.			

Review the form with some of the Key People in your life. Make any adjustments or changes you feel are relevant based on their feedback.

Be Realistic in Your Targets

Set your targets as a stretch, but be realistic with them. They should not be so easy that they do not motivate you, nor should they be set so far away that you know you will never reach them and, therefore, don't bother trying. Take a look at your entire life and decide what you realistically want to achieve.

I used to be a perfectionist. I didn't realize it, but I was striving for straight A's in school, great reviews at work and praise for the perfect dinner party. I had never looked at the targets I had unknowingly set for myself. During a personal development workshop, another participant asked me if I was a perfectionist. I said "No," but the question haunted me all evening. The next morning when the workshop resumed I amended my answer to the question. I learned quite a lot about myself through that question and with the support of the group learned to set "less than perfect" goals. Instead of worrying about dust on the furniture and a culinary delight for guests, I now strive to enjoy myself with my guests while accepting a less-than-perfect house. This has taken considerable pressure off me. I enjoy entertaining more, and I have less stress as a result.

So be realistic about your choice of targets – and remember to keep the overall plan for your life in focus. You must make trade-offs in your life. You can spend many hours exercising for health, but it is at the expense of your career and relationships. You have to balance all the parts of your life and choose appropriate targets.

Now take some time to review the Key Success Measures Chart. If you have blanks in the current status column, don't worry. This is normal; if you haven't tracked the Success Measure previously then you won't know what it is right now. One of the things you will do when you create strategies and actions is to review your Success Measure Tracking System. The system will assist you to determine what you must do to move closer to your Ideal Future.

And remember not to strive for perfection. Consider "less than perfect" goals that are more realistic and less stressful.

Reviewing Progress

Now that you've set some long-term targets for your Success Measures, you will need to track your progress towards these targets through the use of **some of the everyday magic - an annual check up and quarterly reviews**. You should be setting annual targets for each measurement area and then regularly checking your actual results against these yearly goals.

During the year, **life will happen**. This means that things will not be exactly as you had planned. That's all right. You should regularly check what you have actually achieved against the Success Measures, if there is a difference between them you have some choices:

> When there's a difference between what you've achieved and your target, you must determine what to do to bring the two in line:
>
> - Implement some new actions
> - Modify what you are already doing
> - Change your target

The first choice you have if there is a difference between your target and your results is to *add some new actions*. These actions will help you close the gap between where you are and where you want to be. They will be actions that will impact the Success Measures so that you move closer to your targets. This could mean adding something like a woodworking or yoga class to your schedule.

You could also *modify what you are already doing*. For example, you could do more or less of something that you are already doing. You could volunteer at your children's school twice per month instead of once or you could reduce the amount of commuting time by leaving the house earlier each morning. By making changes to something you are already doing you will help your progress move more quickly towards the target.

The final option is to *change your target*. This option is the last one because I want you to think about different ways of reaching your target before just changing it. However, you must also be realistic about what you can achieve, so if you have seriously considered the other two options then changing the target could be the thing for you to do.

Tracking Chart

The following chart is one way to track your progress in each measurement area. It will serve as a way to quickly monitor progress in the many areas of your life.

Complete the Tracking Chart as best you can today:

Success Measure	Current Status	Intermediate Targets								Target	
		Year 1		Year 2		Year 3		Year 4			
		Actual	Target	Actual	Target	Actual	Target	Actual	Target	Actual	Target
1.											
2.											
3.											
4.											
5.											
6.											
7.											
8.											
9.											
10.											

Your completed Success Measure Tracking System will become your report card for quarterly reviewing your Key Success Measures. By regularly reviewing your progress, you will gain a clear picture of how well you are doing and what changes in strategy and action you need to make.

Showing Progress

The only way to know if you are making progress towards your **Extraordinary Life** is through measurement. Choose measures that will show you where you can make small changes that have a large benefit, instead of waiting and realizing too late that something needs to be done.

Remember that you have many parts of your life, so measure from some of the more important areas and be realistic in the targets that you choose.

It is important to monitor your Success Measures throughout the year, not just once each year. Also remember that you can change your measures and targets if they don't give you an early enough warning or are too easy or difficult to achieve.

6

Creating Strategies:

What Should I Do to Create Magic?

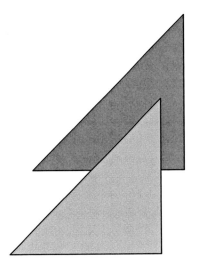

Creating Strategies:

What Should I Do to Create Magic?

The first step to a great life is to fill your life with a positive faith
that will help you through anything.
The second is to begin where you are.

- Dr. Norman Vincent Peale

You have made remarkable progress by advancing this far in the book. I am thrilled by your achievements to date you should be too!

We are now going to create strategies for living your purpose. Before you decide on our actions to take you are going to have to take a look at where you are now in terms of living an Extraordinary Life. Before we can build the bridge to get us to our Ideal Future, we need to know where we are now.

You may want to skip over this step if you think you already know yourself well enough. However, if you are building a bridge to cross the gulf between where you are and where you want to be, you must be very sure of your current position before you start pouring the foundations. Starting with your current situation ensures you develop effective strategies to create this bridge.

So for those of you who want to "get into the action," please stay with me for this section. It's critical that you know yourself well to ensure you *create magic* in your life.

Assessment - *Where Am I Now?*

To know yourself is an unusual and valuable gift. Often we see ourselves as we would like to be instead of who we really are. It is important to spend some time truly understanding where we are today – who we are, what are our strengths and skills and what are our weaknesses and warts. Walter Anderson says, *"Our lives improve only when we take chances – and the first and most difficult risk we can take is to be honest with ourselves."* Then, the next step is truly accepting who you are.

I often find myself looking ahead into the future, thinking about an event next week or next month instead of reveling in where I am now. I get much enjoyment from planning a trip, perhaps more or as much as being there. Instead of **"smelling the roses"** I am dreaming of something that hasn't even happened. One of the best pieces of advice I received was from a counselor about 20 years ago when I was going through a divorce. She said not to understand the myriad of feelings and options, but to just experience the feelings at that moment and to acknowledge them. I needed to be aware of the present before I could move forward.

Tools

There are many tools available to honestly assess where you are today - your Current State. We are going to use the following assessments that I have used successfully in the past:

- **Life Circle – How you divide up your time and energy**
- **Supports and Challenges – What can help or hinder you**
- **SWOT – Strengths, Weaknesses, Opportunities and Threats**

Remember: **"honesty is the best policy."** Be as honest as possible when assessing your current situation. It is only through really understanding ourselves that we can help others and ourselves.

In his book, *"Good to Great"*, Jim Collins describes the paradox of being focused on living your mission while still being brutally honest about how things are now: *"You must maintain unwavering faith that you can and will prevail in the end, regardless of the difficulties, AND at the same time have the discipline to confront the most brutal facts of your current reality, whatever they may be."*

Life Circle

We all know that we have a limited amount of time and energy in our lives. We continually make choices about how we spend these precious resources. However, we are not always aware that we have choices. For example, most of us really can choose to quit our job if we are unhappy, even though most of us would say we couldn't. We would throw out lots of reasons why we couldn't: loss of income, the need to support our families, etc., even though we are unchallenged and uncommitted at work. But the truth is we can quit *if we choose to do so.* We know we really do have other options – but we choose to stay because we are scared or don't like the possible consequences of the decision.

Let's look at where you choose to spend your time and energy. Allow the circle below to represent your life. You are going to designate slices of the circle that are proportional to the amount of time or energy you spend on each area. Each slice will look like a slice from an apple pie, except the slices are probably not all the same size. Each slice of the pie will be sized to show how much time and effort each part of your life represents. This doesn't mean the time or energy you would *like* to spend, but how it actually is *now*.

The best way to complete this exercise is to think of a typical week or month. The exercise is even more powerful if you have the actual data from a typical week or month. Think about all of the possible slices of your life: exercise or sports, learning, working, your relationship, parenting, volunteer work, meditating, planning, sleeping, entertainment, commuting, housework, travel, reading, errands, shopping, finances, friendships, school, grooming, chauffeuring, relaxing, hobbies, spiritual practices, etc.

- **Draw and label the slices that represent how you spend your time and energy at the present time:**

PRESENT

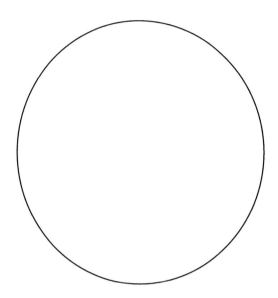

- **Review the slices of your circle.** Do they represent all the parts of your life? Do you have any time for unscheduled events like a sick parent or child, an automobile repair or a friend in need? What gives when unscheduled events occur? Do you have any time to discover every day magic – like listening to the rain on the roof, blowing dandelion seeds with a child or watching a bird soar? What things can you say "no" to, what can you eliminate or reduce? Is there time for you? **Write down your reflections.**

- **Now review Your Ideal Future from** *Chapter 4 - Defining an Extraordinary Life*. What would the slices of your life circle look like if you were living that Extraordinary Life? Remember to include time for unscheduled events and magic. Also include time for doing the things you need to maintain your energy level – physical, intellectual and spiritual. **Draw and label the slices that represent how you would spend your time and energy if you were living your Extraordinary Life:**

FUTURE

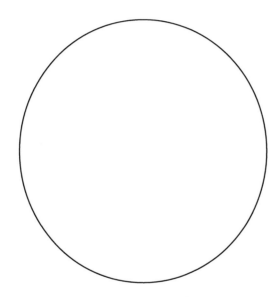

- **Capture your reflections on the differences between today's life circle and your desired life circle:**

Supports and Challenges

When you undertake any changes in your life, there are always people, situations and desires available to support us during these times. There are also challenges to our moving forward – or we'd already be there. These challenges can be internal or external forces, occurrences and people.

Hazel

While working full-time in the energy industry, Hazel decided to attend evening classes to achieve her Bachelor's degree. Both supports and challenges existed in Hazel's life as she moved toward achieving her dream. Supports included a great husband who took over the cooking responsibilities, two sons who helped with housecleaning, friends in the same educational program and another friend who could coach her through the dreaded, but required, calculus. Challenges included her own high cleaning standards, doing homework while surrounded by her family, membership in many volunteer organizations, the boys' school challenges, co-workers who talked support but were actually saboteurs and difficulty saying "no" to friends and family.

Hazel had to lower her cleaning standards because the boys did not clean as well as she did, she had to keep focused on her homework even though a fight was ensuing in the next room and she stopped attending her volunteer meetings. She discovered that by continually re-negotiating with her family, she was able to achieve her degree and still be a contributing family member and friend.

Your Supports and Challenges

• When you think about making positive changes in your life, what are some of the people, situations or emotions that will make the changes easier to achieve? Record them here:

- Document some of the challenges, barriers or walls that might cause problems or hinder your movement forward:

SWOT Analysis

The **SWOT Analysis** is a tool that has been used by business and life planners for many years. SWOT stands for Strengths, Weaknesses, Opportunities and Threats.

A SWOT analysis will assist you in determining the gap between where you are and where you want to be. It will also suggest strategies and actions for achieving your desired life. A SWOT analysis describes the situation today, not in the past or the future.

There are two parts to a SWOT – the *internal* and the *external*.

Strengths and Weaknesses are *internal to you*. They make up whom you are. By using both Strengths and Weaknesses you are taking a total look at the way you are today. Some examples of *internal* Strengths or Weaknesses could be your attitude towards the situation, computer skills or ability to manage change.

Opportunities and Threats are *external to you* – those things that might happen to you which are outside. Because Opportunities and Threats are outside of you, they could be an upcoming election, your support network, other people or changes at work.

What you see as a Strength could be perceived by someone else as a Weakness, that's fine because there are no right or wrong answers. For example, I am a talkative person, I perceive this as a Strength when I am giving information on a topic or starting up a conversation, but it can also be a weakness if I am talking instead of listening to someone else's opinion. This assessment is a tool for you to determine how you see yourself and your situation at this moment.

Your SWOT Analysis

Complete the SWOT analysis by answering the questions in the Internal and External tables:

Internal:

Strengths	Weaknesses
What abilities, attitudes, skills and knowledge do you possess that you and others consider your strengths?	What areas could you improve upon?

External:

Opportunities	Threats
What is happening or might happen in your world that could indicate a positive change? What have you read about, talked about or heard rumors about that you think might have a positive impact on you?	What might happen that could turn your world upside down? What could occur that you perceive as negative?

Your answers from the three assessments will be used in the next section to help you decide on which strategies to choose.

Strategy Development - *Mind the Gap*

I used to ride the train to work and at every station I heard a recorded voice telling me to "mind the gap" - the space between the train and the platform. Due to the daily repetition that phrase still rings in my head as I think about moving forward towards an **Extraordinary Life**.

I know that a gap exists between your current life and the life you want to live (or else you wouldn't be reading this book). So together we're going to "mind the gap."

Define the Gap

In order to define the gap you must know the two end points – where you want to be and where you are now.

You have already defined the life you want to live and your current situation. On the next page under the column titled *"My Extraordinary Life"* **record the highlights of your mission and values from** *Chapter 4 - Defining an Extraordinary Life* **and your desired life in the** *Life Circle* **assessment in this chapter.**

Under the column titled *"Current Situation"* **capture the highlights from the three assessments from the previous section:** *Life Circle, Supports and Challenges* **and** *SWOT* **plus** *Critical Issues, Barriers* **and** *Decision Making Questionnaire* **from** *Chapter 3 - Remembering the Outside World.*

Review what you have written under *"My Extraordinary Life"* **and** *"Current Situation"*. **In the column between them, called** *"Gap,"* **document the differences between your current life and the life you want to live.** This is the gap we will address through strategies.

My Extraordinary Life	Gap	Current Situation

Core Strategies - *Addressing the Gap*

Core strategies are four to six "buckets of action" that you will implement, with the support of your family and friends, to help you move towards your Ideal Future. These strategies become the structure for all actions and plans you will undertake to live the Extraordinary Life you have defined.

These core strategies will move you towards living a life that sees you living your mission every day in a balanced way: physically, intellectually and spiritually. You will be implementing these strategies over the life of your planning horizon, which is the date you chose in *Chapter 4 - Defining an Extraordinary Life*.

Go back to *Define the Gap* **in this chapter. Review your description of your Extraordinary Life, your current situation and the ensuing gap.** Your four to six core strategies will address this gap. These core strategies are the groupings of actions that will move you towards that Extraordinary Life over the planning horizon, taking into account your Current State Assessment and learnings from *Chapter 3 -Remembering the Outside World*.

Making Difficult Choices

Many people find it difficult to reduce all they want to achieve into a few core strategies. Like Elton John sings in *"The Circle of Life"*: *"From the day we arrive on the planet and blinking step into the sun, there's more to be seen than can ever be seen, more to do than can ever be done."* There are many options for you, but you cannot do all of them, you have to make choices about what you are going to do in your Extraordinary Life and what you are not going to achieve. It may not be an easy choice but I have found that very successful people focus on a few important goals and make progress on those. If you try to work on too many strategies at one time, you likely won't see any forward movement, and you will get frustrated and give up. My advice is to choose those few but important strategies that you define as vital during the next few years and work hard on those. Once you've achieved success in those areas, you can work on some of your other goals.

It is difficult to decide what to do to achieve the Extraordinary Life you want. There are many options that will move you forward. You must prioritize – decide what factors are most important in moving you in the direction of your desired goal.

I received some sage advice on prioritization from one of my favorite university professors, Chris Springer. Mr. Springer was one of my favorites because he reached out to each student as an individual instead of a name on a class list. He knew the name of every student, even when there were close to 100 students in each class. I talked to him about the difficulties I was experiencing in doing all of the things I wanted to do: staying timely on homework, living off-campus, writing letters home, having fun, making new friends and keeping up on what was happening in the world.

Professor Springer told me that I had a finite amount of time and energy and I would have to make some choices about how I used those resources as a student. He also said that I would probably make different decisions once I graduated. I decided to write friends and family less often and cancel reading the newspaper but to combine eating supper with watching the evening news. These choices worked well. And he was right; after I finished school, I changed some of those decisions. I try not to eat when the television is on, I call instead of writing home and I read newspapers and magazines once again.

After reviewing my Ideal Future and where I am now, I realized there were many things I wanted to accomplish. However, with limited time, energy and money, I decided that the four main strategies that will best help me achieve my ideal are *Business Development, Building and Maintaining Relationships, Personal and Professional Growth* and *Healthy Lifestyle*. If I complete everything that I want to achieve in these areas, then I can pick up one of the other options I considered but didn't include in Core Strategies.

It is better to complete one strategy or task before completing another. This way you are not in the middle of everything and can focus and thereby see progress through the completion of fewer tasks. You can't do it all at once – although I have a friend who tries to. She "multi-tasks," which means she has about six things going at once. She'd get more accomplished if she did them one at a time instead of a little bit of each of them at the same time. If you are a multi-tasker, I recommend that for one week you attempt to do one thing at a time. Completing one task before starting the next one. At the end of the week compare your effectiveness to when you were trying to do many things at once and I believe that you will see that concentrating on one task at a time is a better use of your energies.

Core Strategies

Core strategies could include Career Development, Financial Freedom, Exercise, Improving Relationships, Personal Development, Health Improvement, Community Impact, Spiritual Growth, Seeing More of the World Through Travel, Minimizing Debt, Family Cohesiveness, or Going Back to School.

Write your four to six core strategies here:

1.

2.

3.

4.

5.

6.

Actions

> "First say to yourself what you would be,
> then do what you have to do."
>
> - Epictetus

In order to implement your strategies, you must develop specific actions for each strategy. These actions should be described clearly enough that a stranger would know if you accomplished them or not.

The actions should not be perfect. They should be your *best guess* at the actions you think you should take. During the regular plan "check-ups" you can decide if these actions still serve you or if you should modify them. The thing to do is write them down, try them out and change them if needed.

Martin

A teacher that I admire recently took a very courageous step to help achieve the lifestyle that he and his wife desire. They wanted to experience a new culture and a new language. After almost a quarter century of teaching, Martin decided that a paid year off to pursue his and his wife's dreams would be just the ticket. He discovered that the school board offered "four-over-five" work, meaning he would work for four years, but be paid over five years, with the fifth year as a paid sabbatical. Because his wife was self-employed, she could easily take time off during the sabbatical year. They decided they would both be winners.

During his sabbatical, Martin wants to accomplish three goals: take piano lessons to learn to read music and play Gershwin (he plays the piano beautifully but entirely by ear); travel to southern Europe and India; and "just breathe." He believes his year off will give his "garden," a metaphor for his life, some much-needed fallow time and provide him with more time to plant as well as smell the flowers.

Now, considering your life, list the specific actions, changes, projects and activities under each Core Strategy that will move you forward over the planning horizon towards your definition of an Extraordinary Life. Remember that each action does not have to be a huge leap forward, but a small incremental movement towards the life you desire. Small incremental steps add up into large leaps forward. If actions had to be perfect I would never make progress. Don't strive for perfection but use your best imperfect guess on what will move you a little towards your goals.

Review your Key Success Measures while considering the actions for each Core Strategy. Your Key Success Measures reflect the areas you believe are important to measure from your mission and values. Therefore, there should be actions to impact these measures.

I believe that small changes matter. As the saying goes, *"If you don't believe that small things matter, you've never been in bed with a mosquito."*

Once you have decided upon your actions make a commitment to accomplish them. It is only through commitment that they will leave the paper and bring about positive change. You are responsible for what you do and do not do – don't be a victim of circumstances, choose to **take action!**

Core Strategy Charts

Here is how to complete the Core Strategy charts:

- **Record each Core Strategy at the top of one chart**
- **For each Core Strategy list up to ten actions**
- **For each action, list who is responsible for completing the action in the "Who completes action" column. This responsible person may or may not be you**
- **In the column titled "Other resources required" add any tools, computer programs, money, equipment, people, additional space, etc. that are required to complete the action**
- **Also record the completion date for the action in "Completion Date" column**
- **After you have listed these actions, go back and place an asterisk (*) next to the important actions that have to be completed in the next 12 months**

Core Strategy #1: _____

Actions to be achieved over planning horizon	Who completes action	Other resources required	Completion Date	Status
1.				
2.				
3.				
4.				
5.				
6.				
7.				
8.				
9.				
10.				

Core Strategy #2: _____

Actions to be achieved over planning horizon	Who completes action	Other resources required	Completion Date	Status
1.				
2.				
3.				
4.				
5.				
6.				
7.				
8.				
9.				
10.				

Core Strategy #3: _____

Actions to be achieved over planning horizon	Who completes action	Other resources required	Completion Date	Status
1.				
2.				
3.				
4.				
5.				
6.				
7.				
8.				
9.				
10.				

Core Strategy #4: _____

Actions to be achieved over planning horizon	Who completes action	Other resources required	Completion Date	Status
1.				
2.				
3.				
4.				
5.				
6.				
7.				
8.				
9.				
10.				

Core Strategy #5: _____

Actions to be achieved over planning horizon	Who completes action	Other resources required	Completion Date	Status
1.				
2.				
3.				
4.				
5.				
6.				
7.				
8.				
9.				
10.				

Core Strategy #6: _____

Actions to be achieved over planning horizon	Who completes action	Other resources required	Completion Date	Status
1.				
2.				
3.				
4.				
5.				
6.				
7.				
8.				
9.				
10.				

Annual Work Planning

In the Core Strategy Charts, you have placed an asterisk beside actions that need to be accomplished in the next year. These collective actions are your work plan for the next year. They are the actions that you think will assist you in moving closer to your Extraordinary Life in the next twelve months. **Be realistic on how much you can achieve in the next year - review all the actions with an asterisk and determine if you can really accomplish them in the next twelve months.**

The "Status" column is how you will track your progress on strategies and actions throughout the coming year. Regularly update this column with notes to remind you how things are going on each action. I write "completed," "waiting input from Carla," "started October" or anything else which will help remind me of what is happening on that action.

Review Strategies and Action Plans

In *Remembering the Outside World*, you wrote the names of Key People in your life. These are the people who will support you in the implementation of your strategies and actions.

Review your strategies and action plans with these key people. Ideally, your support system will act, in this case, as a reality check and will also challenge you to make sure you are taking "courageous steps" towards your Extraordinary Life. **After you have finished this review, make any desired updates and adjustments to your strategies and actions.**

Budgeting - *Buying Freedom*

I read an interesting article in the *New York Times* that said that money buys freedom: *"The freedom to do what you want – including, if necessary, telling your boss to drop dead. For non-lottery winners, it's the kind of freedom that comes of thrift and maybe also self-knowledge."* Daniel Akst went on to say something about budgeting that I found fascinating: *"Recognizing that money buys freedom (if not love) might change the way you look at all you make and spend. If you're smart, it will induce you to save more."* So if you want freedom to live an Extraordinary Life, then take a serious look at budgeting.

Budgeting is about deciding where to put your limited financial resources. Budgeting may not be your favorite activity, but you must ensure that your actions and strategies are funded so that they can be accomplished. Without the money, you may have great ideas but they will probably not be completed.

I used to be of the "money grows on trees" school of budgeting until I started dating an accountant. He explained the importance of budgeting to me and helped me develop my own budget. It was a painful experience, but I needed it – if I can budget and survive, so can you! (By the way, I married that accountant and we are still together!)

To create a workable budget, you must first know where your money comes from and where it goes. Do not guess where you money actually goes, use receipts and statements to give you the correct numbers. If you don't know where the undocumented money goes, carry a notepad with you and write down every penny you spend for a week. If you buy a candy bar, then write it down on the notepad. I spent a month writing down every penny I spent and found the exercising enlightening. I was more conscious about my spending decisions when I had to note each purchase in my book. If you are like me, you will be astounded at how much of your hard-earned money is spent in frivolous ways.

Budgeting Plan Form

Using actual expenditures complete the "History" column to show your previous spending habits.

Based upon your expected monthly income, allocate your resources in the "Planned" column among the possible expenses to support your strategies and actions plus your daily living.

Remember to keep a portion of your funds in miscellaneous expenses to cover the unexpected costs. For example, my husband & I donate to charity instead of sending flowers to funerals. We do not know how many of these unfortunate expenditures we will experience in a year but we plan some extra funds for this and other unplanned expenses.

Also remember to carve out your savings prior to planning your other expenses. Many financial experts recommend that an automatic 10% of your income be put in savings prior to paying your bills and expenses. It may seem to be unrealistic but I have discovered that it is a painless way of saving because the money gets taken away before I even think about spending it.

CATEGORY	HISTORY	ACTUAL	PLANNED
INCOME:			
Wages & bonuses			
Investment income			
Miscellaneous income			
INCOME SUBTOTAL			
EXPENSES:			
Mortgage or rent			
Utilities: gas, water, electric, etc.			
Insurance – home, rental, business, auto, etc.			
Telephone, cable, satellite, newspaper, books, magazines			
Entertainment, recreation, hobbies			

Home repairs or maintenance			
Car - payments, repairs, maintenance, fuel			
Miscellaneous transportation – bus, rentals, etc.			
Groceries			
Eating out			
Child care			
Computer expenses			
Health care			
Savings			
Gifts, donations			
Interest expense			
Pets			
Taxes – property, income, etc.			
Laundry, dry cleaning, house cleaners			
Clothing			
Memberships, clubs			
Personal or Professional Development			
Credit card or debt payments			
Travel			
Miscellaneous			
EXPENSES SUBTOTAL			
NET INCOME **(Income subtotal – Expenses subtotal)**			

You will complete the "Actual" column throughout the year when you have real data about how you are spending your resources compared to your planned expenditures.

Review the completed Budgeting Plan Form. Are your planned monthly expenses in excess of your planned monthly income? It is not unusual for this to occur. You need to make choices – and these need to be informed choices. You already know where you want your life to go – toward your Ideal Future - and you know what strategies and actions are needed to move towards that ideal. You are also aware of some of the costs associated with those actions from the "Other resources required" column of your Core Strategy Charts.

Reality Check

Now it is time to make some of those choices. **Review the Budgeting Plan Form and your Core Strategy Charts.** Are there any disconnects? Do you have to cut down on some expenses? Do you have to move some actions into the next year? Should you consolidate your debts? Do you need to cut up your credit cards? Should you make an appointment with a financial counselor?

Make the necessary changes to the Budget and Core Strategy Charts. I believe it is better to be realistic in planning than to make plans we have no hope of accomplishing.

Write any actions you must take as a result of reviewing the Budgeting Plan Form here:

Preparing for Success - *How Will I Manage the Changes?*

Starting to implement the strategies and actions to live an Extraordinary Life will be a change to how you are living now. It will be an adjustment, but one that is worthwhile. When you get off the treadmill you need to be prepared for stepping onto the floor and making real progress forward.

If you are like most people, you are uncomfortable with change. I am not just uncomfortable with change, I actually dislike it. I remember traveling to our cottage for the first time each spring and being disappointed that the ice and water had changed the sandy shoreline yet again. I wanted this summer's shore to look exactly the same as it did last year. I liked last year's beach and didn't want it to be different. I am not much different than that little girl, however, I now expect change and accept that things are going to be different. I remember that if I am moving towards a life full of **magic** that the changes will mostly be for the better.

Some people think preparing for implementation is unnecessary, but the majority of plans are not put into practice because the procedures, systems and processes to ensure successful implementation were not in place. I want you to succeed, to *"work your plan,"* and the best way I know to ensure that you successfully act upon your plan is to invest some time preparing for that implementation.

The Rollercoaster of Change^{SM}

"Change is not only likely, it's inevitable."

- Barbara Sher

But before you begin planning for implementation, you must understand change. Change is the process people experience when they turn from the comfortable "old" state to a "new" or different state. The comfortable "old" state is what we've been calling the current state, with your current situation, life, problems and concerns. The "new" state is the Extraordinary Life you described through your Mission and Values.

Everyone experiences the same change dynamics – whether we choose the "new" state or whether it is forced upon us. The change experience can feel like you are riding a rollercoaster of emotions – up and down and out of control.

The Rollercoaster of Change^{SM} is *The Centre for Strategic Management's* model that shows the four basic steps that people go through during change. Each of us experiences these four stages at different intensities and for different periods of time.

The Rollercoaster of Change^{SM}

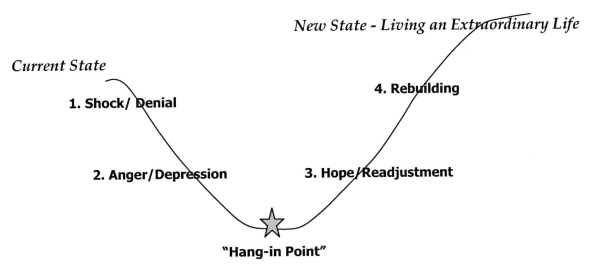

91

Shock/Denial: The first stage I experience during any change is shock and denial – whether the change is one I wanted or whether it was imposed upon me. When my father died suddenly, I was in shock because he had always been an important part of my life. I couldn't believe he was gone. During the Stock/Denial phase many people deny the experience occurred – they pretend that it just didn't happen. They may also feel numb.

Anger/Depression: After I got over the shock and denial, I entered the second stage of the Rollercoaster of Change^{SM} - anger and depression. People in the Anger/Depression stage may also feel confused, unmotivated or that they are just "going through the motions." After I realized my beloved father was actually gone, I felt tired, sad, weighed down - and angry at him for leaving me.

"Hang-in Point": During the anger and depression stage, people hit the *"hang-in point."* This is where people make a decision to either stay on the down side of the change experience or start up the other side. Some people at the "Hang-in Point" choose to exit the situation by leaving their organization or marriage, while others decide to make the best of the new situation and start up the other side of the rollercoaster. A third group chooses to stay at the bottom of the Rollercoaster of Change^{SM}, perpetually living the down side of change. At my "Hang-in Point" I made a decision to move up the other side of the rollercoaster and get on with my life.

Hope/Readjustment: On the upward side of the rollercoaster I experienced the third stage of the Rollercoaster of Change^{SM} - hope and readjustment. I realized that my father would always be in my heart and that the love and learnings don't disappear when one of us dies. In this stage, people start to realize that the new state could be a good place to be. As Ghandi put it: *"If you want to change the world, start by being that change."* I began to try new behaviors and I gained new energy.

Rebuilding: Finally, I began to rebuild and accept the new state. I may not like the fact that my father passed away earlier than I had hoped, but I know he loved me and our family and he is gone to a better place. In this final stage of the Rollercoaster of Change^{SM} people become accustomed to the "new" state and start living an Extraordinary Life.

Change Survival Pack

We have all experienced change in our lives. Some of the changes were for the better, some were not; some changes we chose and some we did not. Because you have survived change in the past, you have already accumulated experiences and ideas for your own Change Survival Pack. The following story and questions will help you determine what you have in your Change Survival Pack so that you can use these experiences again for upcoming changes.

Liz

Liz is a successful manager in a growing organization. She was unexpectedly widowed, leaving her with two young children. When she found out about her husband's death she was in shock. No one could believe he was gone. After the shock wore off, she was angry at being left alone to raise two boys under the age of six, but with the support of friends and family and her own positive attitude she began to adjust to her life and create new dreams for the future. Liz used many techniques for managing the stress of the sudden loss of her husband: she talked to friends, exercised regularly and made her sons her first priority for the first few years. Her life now is not what she expected it would be ten years ago, but she is happy, is a great parent and has recently remarried.

Your Change Survival Pack

1. What changes have you been through in your life?

2. Write examples of what you experienced during the four basic stages of the Rollercoaster of Change^{SM}. Also record what you did at each stage to help move through this change cycle.

Stages of the Rollercoaster of Change^{SM}	What I experienced	What I did to move through the Rollercoaster of Change^{SM}
Shock/Denial		
Anger/Depression		
Hope/Readjustment		
Rebuilding		

3. What has helped you manage change effectively in the past?

4. Who or what has supported you through past changes?

5. How do you reduce and manage stress?

6. What have you learned from the past that will help you go through the changes associated with implementing your strategies and actions?

7. What rewards or reinforcers have you used to keep you motivated during change?

Managing Change

"Observe that all things take place by change
and consider that the nature of the Universe loves nothing so much
as to change the things which are."

- Marcus Aurelius

Review your answers to the questions from *"Your Change Survival Pack"* **and in the chart below document how you will help yourself manage the changes associated with moving towards your Extraordinary Life:**

What To Do	Resources Needed	Others Involved	Completion Date
1.			
2.			
3.			

In order to successfully make the changes in your life, you need to be ready for those changes. Change occurs all of the time, but yet we often resist change. I once read that the only person who likes change is a wet baby. That may be so, but if change is going to happen to us, I think we should understand it better.

Change is a psychological process that each one of us experiences differently based upon who we are and what our experiences are. The Rollercoaster of Change[SM] shows us the stages that we all go through during change – whether it's a small change like misplacing a book or something large like the loss of a job. If the journey through change is not pleasant, then we can shorten the time spent on the journey through planning for the change.

7

Ensuring Success:

How Do I Use Ordinary Magic to Live an Extraordinary Life?

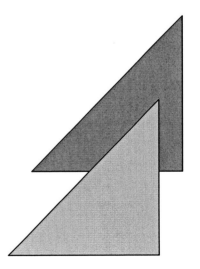

Ensuring Success:

How Do I Use Ordinary Magic to Live an Extraordinary Life?

"The butterfly becomes only when it's entirely ready."

- Chinese proverb

You now have strategies and actions that will move you along the path from where you are to an Extraordinary Life. **Congratulations!** You've accomplished a great deal of hard work and should give yourself a pat on the back. At this point, however, many people want to brush off their hands and close the book. But hang in there! Only about 20% of the work is done – you now have to implement the strategies and actions you have worked so hard to create. You must turn your written strategies and action plans into real actions.

Now here's the bad news: *this is where most people fail*. Many of us are great with ideas, but when it comes to implementation we run out of energy. However, we can combat this by the use of ordinary magic.

Ordinary magic is things that are easily available to you that will help you live your plan – just like magic. The ordinary magic that is around you without extra cost is writing the plan down, getting support from others and monthly monitoring.

These easy actions of writing, receiving support and monitoring don't sound very magic to people. But they do work like magic to ensure that you steadily make progress towards living an Extraordinary Life. A life full of purpose and magic.

Taking Action - *Using Ordinary Magic*

Writing your plan on paper, sharing with your Key People for support and checking monthly seem quite ordinary. However, they are the magic that ensures you take action – that the plan doesn't sit in a drawer somewhere forgotten, but instead you take the plan and build your Extraordinary Life with it.

Frank and I worked with a builder to create our home. We spent hours pouring over the plans on paper, but the plans were not the house. The builder had to take action – build the house. We visited the site daily to monitor the progress and found some errors that were easy to fix during the building stage but would have been costly to rectify after the house was built. This is the same idea for building your Extraordinary Life. You need to create a plan, get support from others and regularly monitor your progress.

> Here is the ordinary magic we can use to ensure success:
>
> - **Write it down** – Create a plan
> - **Get support** – From the Key People in your life
> - **Monitor regularly** – Monthly review of progress

Write It Down

The act of committing your plan to paper is difficult for many of us. This is because before we write it down, our plan is still a dream and therefore we can't fail. If I only keep the plan in my head then it is still possible to achieve, but by committing it to paper I must either fail or succeed. Compounding this is the fact that many of us have a fear of failure - creating a plan is the first step in actually doing something and this could lead to failure. But remember that *not* putting your plan down on paper is a sure way of failing to reach your goals.

It might be frightening and uncomfortable, but I encourage you to go ahead and create a plan. Don't try to write a perfect plan. It can be modified and changed, but please start somewhere. Here's an idea of what your **Extraordinary Life Plan** might look like:

An Extraordinary Life Plan:

Introduction   1-3 pages
- Background, Key People in My Life, Issues and Barriers, Future External Scan, Systems Thinking Approach[SM]

An Extraordinary Life   1-2 pages
- Mission, Values

Tracking Progress   1 page
- Success Measures

Creating Strategies   2-6 pages
- Core Strategies and Actions, Budget

Ensuring Success   1 page
- Managing Change, Schedule of Plan Reviews

Appendix   2-3 pages
- Mission and Values Background and Drawings; Current State Assessment – Life Circle, Supports and Challenges, SWOT Analysis, Define the Gap

TOTAL   8-16 pages

This may seem like many pages. The entire plan takes quite a bit of thought, but the main parts of the **Extraordinary Life Plan** that you can "pull out" and keep close by for regular checking are *1.) Success Measures* and *2.) Core Strategies and Actions*. These few pages are the heart of the **Extraordinary Life Plan**. They will help guide your decisions because imbedded in them are all the other thinking you've done around where you want to go and where you are now.

I have included my **Extraordinary Life Plan** in **Appendix A** to give you a guide to follow when you are creating your own **Extraordinary Life Plan**.

Get Support

Many people find it difficult to ask for help or support, yet are often the first to assist others. I don't like asking for help. Sometimes I think it makes me look weak or not capable of handling things. On the contrary, asking for assistance from the Key People in my life means that I can accomplish more with their support, I can become more knowledgeable and even more skilled. I believe that now is a good time to give yourself permission to ask for support and help from the Key People in your life. People want to help the people that are in their life. Most of the Key People will be pleased that they were asked and will make the implementation of your plan easier.

Share your plan with your support network. Ask them for ideas on how they can support you throughout the implementation of your plan. You may want to set up regular visits or phone calls to keep your momentum moving forward.

I get support from my husband, family and friends, but sometimes they can be "too nice"; sometimes I need a push. So I have hired a coach to help me make progress towards my definition of an Extraordinary Life. We meet once per month to discuss actions for the month that will move me towards fulfilling my life purpose. We discuss exercise, nutrition, work, personal and professional growth, stress and connection to spirit. I send him regular email updates on my actions. He supports me through emails and telephone calls between meetings. I have found that this structure allows me to take *"big steps"* forward, steps that a friend or family member might not push me towards.

Monitor Regularly

When things are new and exciting, my motivation level is high. However, once I am back in the midst of life, some of that motivation can wear off. I have discovered that the best way to keep my motivation level up is to regularly monitor my progress. For example, you could set up a monthly check-in with one of your support people.

Who of us is truly perfect? I know that I am not. I am always re-evaluating and making minor adjustments because events are always changing around me. Therefore, the most important aspect of achieving an Extraordinary Life is in the being, in the doing, in living and in striving each day.

Annual Review and Update - *What Can I Do to Stay Motivated?*

"You are never given a wish without also being given
the power to make it true.
You may have to work for it, however."

- Richard Bach

Achieving long-term success means that you must be vigilant in the application of your plan and you need to update it annually. This Annual Review and Update is an opportunity for you to refine, revisit and recommit by reviewing all parts of your plan:

- **Phase A – Defining an Extraordinary Life**
  - o Mission
  - o Values

- **Phase B – Tracking Progress**
  - o Key Success Measures

- **Phase C – Creating Strategies**
  - o Current State Assessment
  - o Minding the Gap
  - o Core Strategies and Actions
  - o Budgeting

- **Phase D – Ensuring Success**
  - o Write It Down
  - o Get Support
  - o Monitor Regularly

- **Phase E – Remembering the Outside World**
  - o Future External Scan

During the Annual Review and Update, you will determine what has changed in your environment, what progress you have achieved and what refinements need to be made to your plan. Once the plan has been updated, you and your support network can then recommit to the plan.

I update my **Extraordinary Life Plan** annually. It is an excellent opportunity to not only review my plan, but also to celebrate my accomplishments. I get to see the progress that I have made throughout the year by looking at what I've achieved in my Annual Workplan. When I am working day-to-day I don't see the strides that I have made, so the Annual Review and Update gives me the space to look at the big picture. I tend to treat myself well when doing the review and update. My husband, Frank, and I have updated our Plans at a golf course in the Rocky Mountains, at a historic B&B, in busy London and on the coast of the Gulf of Mexico. I find that being away from home allows us to focus on the update plus celebrate our progress.

You may not be able to travel to review your Annual Review and Update. But try to get away from the phone, meetings, children, etc. in order to concentrate on reviewing your accomplishments, updating your plan for the next year and celebrating your successes.

Remember to congratulate yourself on your accomplishments. A celebration that includes the Key People in your support network will not only thank those people for their contribution, but also remind them of your next steps together.

Congratulations and Good Luck!

It is time for congratulations on the completion of your **Extraordinary Life Plan**! You have taken a courageous step forward in living a life full of magic and purpose.

I congratulate you on the investment of time and effort to create your Plan. You have taken the first important step towards creating the life you desire.

Implementation of the **Extraordinary Life Plan** is next. I wish you much luck on the successful realization of your plan. Keep up with the monitoring and measuring, it is worth it!

Please send me an email with your success stories through my website at **www.valeriemacleod.com**.

Best of luck in achieving the life you dream of!

May your hopes and dreams be carried on eagles' wings!

Extraordinary Life Plan

Updated 2004

Appendix A

Extraordinary Life Plan

Updated 2004

Mission

I was put on the planet to guide people to find their own answers. I am an educator, facilitator, coach and guide. I am a successful business consultant with a well-oiled, client satisfying, money-generating business. I make meaningful investments and contributions to the community. I am healthy, connected to God and have great relationships with my husband, family and friends.

Values

Integrity – Honesty and Congruence

Balance – Living all facets of my life

Personal and Professional Growth – Continuous learning and improvement

Harmony – Building common ground

Feedback – *Key Success Measures*

Key Success Measures:

1. **Business Development**

   - # paid days worked per month
   - # follow-up/relationship building calls per month
   - monthly consulting income

2. **Building and Maintaining Relationships**

   - # dates with spouse per month
   - # days worked per week

3. **Personal and Professional Growth**

   - # vacation days per year
   - # days in professional development

4. **Healthy Lifestyle**

   - # hours exercised each week

Key Success Measures Chart

Success Meaures	Current Status	Intermediate Targets								Target Year 5	
		Year 1		Year 2		Year 3		Year 4			
		Actual	Target	Actual	Target	Actual	Target	Actual	Target	Actual	Target
1. Business Development • # paid days per month • # follow-up/relationship building calls per month • monthly consulting income											
2. Building and Maintaining Relationships • # dates with spouse per month • # days worked per week											
3. Personal and Professional Growth • # vacation days per year • # days in professional development											
4. Healthy Lifestyle • # hours exercised each week											

Core Strategies

Strategy #1: Business Development

- Increase potential client base and maintain relationships with existing clients

Strategy #2: Building and Maintaining Relationships

- Continue to improve personal relationships

Strategy #3: Personal and Professional Growth

- Undertake development in both work-related and non-work related arenas

Strategy #4: Healthy Lifestyle

- Maintain an active, nutritionally-balanced lifestyle

Annual Work Plan

Strategy #1: Business Development

- Increase potential client base and maintain relationships with existing clients

Actions to be achieved over planning horizon	Who completes action	Other resources required	Completion Date	Status
1. Make weekly follow-up calls	Valerie	Contact list	Weekly	Ongoing
2. Join board of networking group and invest an average of 3 hours/month	Valerie	Annual dues ($500-$2,000)	January 1	Completed
4. Make monthly calls to potential clients as per marketing plan	Valerie	Leads	Monthly	
4. Investigate co-presenting at conference with client	Valerie	Client time	March 1	Completed
5. Write and publish new book	Valerie		2006	Not started

Strategy #2: Building and Maintaining Relationships

- Continue to improve personal relationships

Actions to be achieved over planning horizon	Who completes action	Other resources required	Completion Date	Status
1. Date spouse once per week	Valerie & Frank		Weekly	Ongoing
2. Talk to mother weekly, visit 3 times every two years	Valerie	$20/mo. $2,000/yr	Monthly	Ongoing
3. Talk to/visit with close friends once per week	Valerie		Weekly	Ongoing
4. Entertain friends every second month	Valerie & Frank		Bi-monthly	Not scheduled

Strategy #3: Personal and Professional Growth

- Undertake development in both work-related and non-work related arenas

Actions to be achieved over planning horizon	Who completes action	Other resources required	Completion Date	Status
1. Attend two professional development workshops or courses/year	Valerie	$2,000 - $5,000	December 1	Completed. Investigate for next year
2. Monthly - order books from Recommended Reading List from public library website	Valerie	Web access, library card	Monthly	Monthly
3. Read journals & magazines monthly	Valerie	$50/mo.	Monthly	Going well for short journals
4. Attend one non-work workshop/year	Valerie	$1,000	September 30	Not scheduled

Strategy #4: Healthy Lifestyle

- Maintain an active, nutritionally-balanced lifestyle

Actions to be achieved over planning horizon	Who completes action	Other resources required	Completion Date	Status
1. Exercise 4 times per week	Valerie	Pool schedule, walking shoes, treadmill	Weekly	Ongoing
2. Maintain good eating habits: Eat breakfast, eat fresh vegetables, increase water, reduce fat	Valerie		Daily	Ongoing
3. Schedule 2-half days off per week	Valerie		Weekly	Ongoing
4. Schedule vacations	Valerie & Frank	Money & time	Quarterly	Research for next year

Managing Change

What To Do	Resources Needed	Others Involved	Completion Date
1. Track implementation of actions when completing monthly business report	Calendar		Monthly
2. Annual review and update on vacation		Frank	Annual
3. Continue working with coach for feedback and goal setting in business; relationships; personal & professional growth; and healthy lifestyle		Coach	Monthly
4. Be aware of energy level and reward myself for accomplishments	Time		Daily

B

Systems Thinking Approach^{SM}:

An Orientation to Life

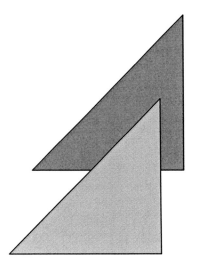

Get Me Off the Treadmill!

Appendix B

Systems Thinking Approach^{SM}:

An Orientation to Life

Systems Thinking is a method of thinking backwards. It originated from the scientific discipline called General Systems Theory, which studies living systems in the world, their relationships and the common laws governing systems. Based on the study of biology in the 1920s, General Systems Theory focused on the *"whole"* of the system prior to the parts. Systems Thinking is the way that all living systems, including you and I, work.

Systems Thinking is the basis for our work at *The Centre for Strategic Management*. It is a holistic approach to seeing the big picture first and then the fit with the pieces.

The Systems Thinking Approach^{SM} will be our map, our navigational tool, as we journey together to create your Extraordinary Life, balanced between the physical, intellectual and spiritual elements. We'll start our journey by determining what you desire in life, where you want to go, and how you'd like your life to be – your Ideal Future. After we have visualized your exciting future, we create feedback mechanisms to ensure that we remain on the path to that envisioned goal.

The third step in the Systems Thinking Approach^{SM} is to determine where we are now – our current situation, problems, concerns and fears. Once we know where we want to go and where we are today, we then create and implement a plan to get from here to our Ideal Future. We can't forget that we live in a changing world, so we will also perform future External Scanning. This will help us determine what is changing or could change in our future that might affect the achievement of our goals.

As you can see in the diagram, The Systems Thinking Approach^{SM} is a circle. You can enter it at any point in the cycle – but the best place is at your Ideal Future.

The Systems Thinking Approach^{SM}

The Systems Thinking Approach^{SM} is built upon five elements:

> **A** – Output
> **B** – Feedback
> **C** – Input
> **D** – Throughput
> **E** – Environment

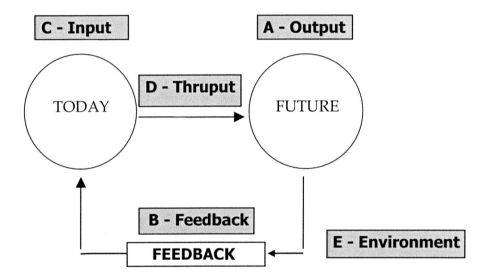

Systems: a set of components that work together for the benefit of the whole.

The Systems Thinking Approach^SM Questions:

A – Output (Defining an Extraordinary Life) refers to where you want to be at a point in the future, what you want your life to look like. The question to ask is: *"If I'm Not on a Treadmill, What Am I Doing?"*

B – Feedback (Tracking Progress) deals with monitoring your movement towards your desired point in the future. It measures or tracks your progress by asking the questions: *"Am I Moving Ahead? Am I on the Right Road?"*

C – Input (Creating Strategies) is the information that helps you determine where you are right now and what to do to move forward. It is the starting point for your journey. You determine input by asking the question: *"What Should I Do to Create Magic?"*

D – Throughput (Ensuring Success) is the application of the strategies to move you from where you are now (Input) to where you want to be (Output). It answers the question: *"How Do I Use Ordinary Magic to Live an Extraordinary Life?"*

E – Environment (Remembering the Outside World) is the ever-changing world around us. It can help or hinder your progress towards your Extraordinary Life. The question to ask yourself is: *"How Will External Changes Affect Me?"*

ISBN 141201693-2